I0844621

TABLE OF CONTENTS

Chapter 1: Foundations of Financial Literacy
- The Importance of Financial Education
- Understanding Budgeting and Saving
- Debunking Common Financial Myths

Chapter 2: Investing Demystified
- The Power of Compound Interest
- Exploring Different Investment Vehicles (Stocks, Bonds, Real Estate, etc.)
- Risk Management and Diversification

Chapter 3: Building a Solid Financial Future
- Setting Clear Financial Goals
- Strategies for Debt Management
- Creating an Effective Emergency Fund

Chapter 4: The Psychology of Money
- Overcoming Financial Anxiety
- Developing a Healthy Relationship with Money

- Behavioral Biases and their Impact on Financial Decisions

Chapter 5: Entrepreneurship and Wealth Creation
- Navigating the World of Entrepreneurship
- Scaling a Business for Profitability
- Innovations in the Digital Age

Chapter 6: Real Estate Riches
- Real Estate Investment Strategies
- Maximizing Rental Income
- Flipping Properties for Profit

Chapter 7: Retirement Planning and Wealth Preservation
- Exploring Retirement Account Options
- Estate Planning and Inheritance Management
- Strategies for Long-Term Wealth Preservation

Chapter 8: Achieving Financial Freedom
- Building Multiple Streams of Income
- Balancing Work and Life for Long-Term Success

- Strategies for Early Retirement

Chapter 9: Navigating Economic Ups and Downs
- Thriving in a Volatile Market
- Adapting to Economic Changes
- Turning Crises into Opportunities

Chapter 10: Inspiring Success Stories
- Interviews with Self-Made Millionaires and Billionaires
- Lessons from Ordinary Individuals who Achieved Extraordinary Wealth
- Actionable Takeaways from Real-Life Examples

Chapter 1: Foundations of Financial Literacy

The Importance of Financial Education

Financial education is the cornerstone of achieving long-term financial well-being and success. It equips individuals with the knowledge, skills, and confidence needed to make informed and effective financial decisions. Here's why financial education is of paramount importance:

1. Empowerment and Confidence: Financial education empowers individuals to take control of their financial lives. When people understand financial concepts, they feel more confident in managing their money, setting financial goals, and making strategic decisions.

2. Smart Decision-Making: Informed individuals are better equipped to make smart financial choices. They can evaluate various options, such as investments, loans, and savings plans, and choose the ones that align with their goals and risk tolerance.

3. Debt Management: Financial education helps people understand the implications of borrowing and how to manage debt responsibly. This knowledge can prevent individuals from falling into cycles of high-interest debt and promote healthier financial habits.

4. Investment and Wealth Creation: A solid understanding of investing principles allows individuals to grow their wealth over time. Financial education teaches concepts like compounding, asset allocation, and risk management, enabling individuals to make informed investment decisions.

5. Risk Mitigation: Financial education helps individuals recognize and manage financial risks. Whether it's insurance, emergency

funds, or understanding economic cycles, being financially educated helps mitigate potential setbacks.

6. Retirement Planning: Understanding retirement savings vehicles and strategies ensures individuals are adequately prepared for their golden years. Financial education encourages early and consistent retirement planning.

7. Entrepreneurship: For aspiring entrepreneurs, financial education provides insights into funding, budgeting, cash flow management, and financial projections. This knowledge is crucial for launching and sustaining a successful business.

8. Economic Citizenship: Financially educated individuals contribute to a stronger economy. They make informed consumption choices, support local businesses, and engage with financial institutions more effectively.

9. Breaking the Cycle: Financial education can break the cycle of poverty and promote

upward social mobility. It equips individuals with the tools to make informed decisions and build a better financial future for themselves and their families.

10. Peace of Mind: Knowing how to manage finances reduces stress and anxiety related to money. Financially educated individuals can navigate unexpected financial challenges with more resilience and peace of mind.
In a world of increasingly complex financial products and options, financial education is not just a luxury; it's a necessity. It empowers individuals to make choices that align with their goals, values, and circumstances, ultimately leading to greater financial security and prosperity.

Understanding Budgeting and Saving

Understanding budgeting and saving is essential for achieving financial stability and realizing your long-term financial goals.
Here's a breakdown of these crucial concepts:

Budgeting:

Budgeting is the process of creating a plan for how you will allocate your income to cover your expenses, savings, and investments. It involves tracking your income, categorizing your expenses, and ensuring that your spending aligns with your financial priorities. Here's how to approach budgeting:

1. Calculate Your Income: Determine your total monthly income from all sources, including your job, investments, and any other sources of revenue.

2. List Your Expenses: Make a comprehensive list of all your regular expenses, including fixed costs (rent/mortgage, utilities) and variable costs (groceries, entertainment).

3. Categorize Expenses: Divide your expenses into categories, such as housing, transportation, food, entertainment, and savings.

4. Set Priorities: Allocate funds to each expense category based on their importance.

Ensure that essentials like housing and utilities are covered first.

5. Track and Adjust: Regularly track your actual spending and compare it to your budget. Adjust your budget as needed to stay on track and accommodate changes in your financial situation.

Saving:
Saving involves setting aside a portion of your income for future use, emergencies, or specific financial goals. It's a critical step in building financial security and achieving your aspirations. Here's how to approach saving:

1. Emergency Fund: Start by building an emergency fund that covers three to six months' worth of living expenses. This fund provides a safety net in case of unexpected financial challenges.

2. Automate Savings: Set up automatic transfers from your checking account to a dedicated savings account. This makes saving a consistent and effortless habit.

3. Short-Term Goals: Identify short-term goals, such as a vacation or purchasing a new appliance. Allocate funds towards these goals to avoid accumulating debt for discretionary expenses.

4. Long-Term Goals: Allocate a portion of your savings towards long-term goals, such as buying a home, funding education, or retiring comfortably.

5. Investing: Once you have a sufficient emergency fund and have saved for your short-term goals, consider investing your savings to potentially earn higher returns over time.

6. Review and Adjust: Regularly review your savings goals and progress. Adjust your savings strategy as your financial situation evolves and new goals arise.

Remember, budgeting and saving are ongoing processes that require discipline and periodic adjustments. They provide you with financial freedom, peace of mind, and the ability to achieve your dreams. By understanding and implementing effective budgeting and saving practices, you can take control of your financial future.

Debunking Common Financial Myths

Let's debunk some common financial myths that often lead to misconceptions and poor financial decisions:

Myth 1: Carrying a Balance on Your Credit Card Improves Your Credit Score
Reality: Carrying a balance on your credit card doesn't help your credit score; it may actually harm it. It's essential to pay off your credit card balance in full each month to avoid interest charges and demonstrate responsible credit usage.

Myth 2: Renting is Throwing Away Money; Buying a Home is Always Better
Reality: Renting can provide flexibility and may be financially beneficial depending on your situation. Owning a home involves

additional costs like maintenance, property taxes, and interest payments. The decision between renting and buying should be based on your financial goals and circumstances.

Myth 3: You Need a High Income to Invest
Reality: While a higher income can make investing easier, anyone can start investing with even a small amount of money. It's the consistency and time in the market that contribute to investment growth. Start early and focus on a diversified portfolio.

Myth 4: Credit Cards Should Be Avoided at All Costs
Reality: Credit cards can be valuable tools if used responsibly. They help build credit, offer rewards, and provide fraud protection. The key is to pay off the balance in full each month and avoid high-interest debt.

Myth 5: A College Degree Guarantees Financial Success
Reality: While education is important, a degree doesn't guarantee success. Other factors like skills, networking, and

adaptability play a role. It's crucial to consider the potential return on investment for your chosen field of study.

Myth 6: Saving Is Enough; You Don't Need to Invest
Reality: Saving is important, but investing allows your money to grow and potentially outpace inflation. Over the long term, investing can help you achieve your financial goals more effectively.

Myth 7: You Need to Time the Market to Be Successful
Reality: Timing the market is extremely difficult and often leads to poor outcomes. A more effective strategy is to invest consistently over time, ride out market fluctuations, and focus on your long-term goals.
Myth 8: More Income Automatically Equals More Wealth
Reality: It's not just about how much you earn but how you manage and allocate your income. Wise financial decisions, budgeting,

and saving play a bigger role in building wealth than just earning a high income.

Myth 9: You Can Borrow Your Way Out of Debt
Reality: Borrowing more to pay off existing debt often leads to a cycle of increasing debt. It's essential to focus on debt repayment strategies and make a concerted effort to reduce outstanding balances.

Myth 10: Financial Advisors Always Have Your Best Interests in Mind
Reality: Not all financial advisors operate under a fiduciary duty to prioritize your interests. Some may have conflicts of interest. Research and choose an advisor who is transparent, trustworthy, and acts in your best interest.

By dispelling these myths, you can make more informed financial decisions and work towards building a stronger, more secure financial future.

Chapter 2: Investing Demystified

The Power of Compound Interest

The power of compound interest is a remarkable phenomenon that can significantly impact your financial growth over time. Compound interest occurs when you earn interest not only on your initial investment but also on the accumulated interest from previous periods. Here's why compound interest is so powerful:

1. Exponential Growth: Unlike simple interest, where you earn interest only on the principal amount, compound interest allows your investment to grow exponentially. As interest is reinvested and compounds, your money can multiply more rapidly.

2. Snowball Effect: Over time, the compounding effect can lead to a snowball effect, where your investment begins to generate more interest than your initial contribution. This self-reinforcing cycle accelerates your wealth accumulation.

3. Long-Term Impact: Compound interest has the most significant impact over long periods. The earlier you start investing, the more time your money has to compound and grow, allowing you to potentially reach your financial goals sooner.

4. Passive Income: Compound interest can eventually generate a substantial amount of passive income. This can be particularly valuable during retirement, as your

investments continue to grow and provide a consistent income stream.

5. Savings Amplification: Saving consistently and allowing your savings to compound can amplify your wealth-building efforts. Even small contributions can grow into substantial sums over time.

6. Cushion Against Inflation: Compound interest helps your money keep pace with or even outpace inflation, ensuring that your purchasing power remains relatively stable.

7. Reinvestment Potential: Reinvesting dividends and interest earned further enhances the compounding effect, leading to even greater long-term growth.

Here's an illustrative example of the power of compound interest:

Let's say you invest $1,000 at an annual interest rate of 8%. After one year, your investment grows to $1,080. In the second year, you earn 8% interest not just on the initial $1,000, but on the $80 interest earned in the first year. This leads to a total of $1,166.40. Over time, this effect becomes more pronounced, and your investment can experience significant growth.

Compound interest is a fundamental concept in investing and is one of the key drivers of long-term financial success. By understanding and harnessing the power of compound interest, you can make strategic investment decisions that lead to substantial wealth accumulation over time. Remember, the earlier you start, the more you can benefit from the magic of compounding.

Exploring Different Investment Vehicles (Stocks, Bonds, Real Estate, etc.)

Certainly, let's explore different investment vehicles that individuals can consider as part of their investment strategy:

1. Stocks:
- Stocks represent ownership in a company. When you buy shares, you become a

shareholder and potentially benefit from the company's profits and growth.
- Stocks offer the potential for high returns, but they also come with higher volatility and risk.
- Diversification across different industries and sectors can help mitigate risk in stock investing.

2. Bonds:
- Bonds are debt securities issued by governments, municipalities, or corporations. When you buy a bond, you're essentially lending money in exchange for periodic interest payments and the return of the principal amount at maturity.
- Bonds are generally considered lower-risk investments compared to stocks, making them suitable for income generation and capital preservation.

3. Real Estate:
- Real estate involves purchasing property (residential, commercial, or industrial) with the expectation of rental income and potential appreciation in value.

- Real estate investing can provide steady cash flow, tax benefits, and portfolio diversification.
- It requires careful management and may involve higher upfront costs and ongoing responsibilities.

4. Mutual Funds:
- Mutual funds pool money from multiple investors to invest in a diversified portfolio of stocks, bonds, or other assets.
- They offer instant diversification, professional management, and are suitable for investors seeking exposure to various asset classes.

5. Exchange-Traded Funds (ETFs):
- ETFs are similar to mutual funds but trade on stock exchanges. They track specific indices or sectors and offer diversification and flexibility.
- ETFs can be bought and sold throughout the trading day, and they often have lower fees compared to mutual funds.

6. Commodities:

- Commodities include physical goods like gold, silver, oil, and agricultural products.
- They can serve as a hedge against inflation and geopolitical uncertainty, but their value can be influenced by supply and demand dynamics.

7. Retirement Accounts (e.g., 401(k), IRA):
- Retirement accounts offer tax advantages to encourage long-term savings. They can hold various investments like stocks, bonds, and mutual funds.
- Contributions to retirement accounts may be tax-deductible, and earnings can grow tax-deferred or tax-free, depending on the account type.

8. Certificates of Deposit (CDs):
- CDs are time-bound deposits offered by banks with fixed interest rates and maturity dates.
- They offer a safe and predictable return but may have lower potential returns compared to other investments.

9. Peer-to-Peer Lending:

- Peer-to-peer lending platforms connect borrowers with individual lenders. Investors can earn interest by lending money to borrowers.
- It offers the potential for higher returns compared to traditional savings accounts, but it also comes with higher risk.

10. Cryptocurrencies:
- Cryptocurrencies like Bitcoin and Ethereum are digital assets that use blockchain technology.
- They are highly volatile and speculative investments, suitable for those comfortable with higher risk.

It's important to conduct thorough research, assess your risk tolerance, and align your investments with your financial goals and timeline. Diversification across different investment vehicles can help manage risk and optimize your overall portfolio. Consider consulting with a financial advisor to create a well-rounded investment strategy that suits your individual circumstances.

Risk Management and Diversification

Risk management and diversification are crucial strategies for safeguarding your investment portfolio and achieving long-term financial success. Here's a closer look at these concepts:

Risk Management:
Risk management involves identifying, assessing, and mitigating potential risks that could negatively impact your investments. The goal is to protect your capital and minimize the potential for significant losses. Here are key principles of risk management:

1. Understand Your Risk Tolerance: Evaluate your comfort level with risk. Consider factors such as your financial goals, time horizon, and emotional resilience to market fluctuations.

2. Diversification: Spread your investments across different asset classes, industries, and

geographic regions. Diversification reduces the impact of a poor-performing investment on your overall portfolio.

3. Asset Allocation: Determine the ideal mix of asset classes (e.g., stocks, bonds, real estate) based on your risk tolerance and goals. Adjust your allocation over time to maintain the desired level of risk exposure.

4. Risk Assessment: Regularly assess the risk profile of your investments. Be aware of factors that could affect their performance, such as economic conditions, industry trends, and geopolitical events.

5. Emergency Fund: Maintain an emergency fund of cash or liquid assets to cover unexpected expenses and prevent the need to sell investments during downturns.

6. Insurance: Consider insurance options, such as health, life, and disability insurance, to protect against unforeseen events that could impact your financial stability. Diversification:

Diversification involves spreading your investments across different assets to reduce the impact of poor performance in any one investment. It is a fundamental strategy to manage risk and optimize returns. Here's how diversification works:

1. Asset Classes: Invest in a mix of asset classes, such as stocks, bonds, real estate, and commodities. Different assets have varying risk profiles and react differently to market conditions.

2. Sector Diversification: Within each asset class, diversify across different sectors or industries. This helps protect against sector-specific risks.

3. Geographic Diversification: Consider investments in different countries and regions to reduce exposure to the economic and political conditions of a single location.

4. Individual Investments: Diversify within each asset class by holding a variety of individual investments. For example, own

stocks from different companies rather than concentrating your investment in one stock.

5. Time Diversification: Invest consistently over time, regardless of market conditions. This strategy, known as dollar-cost averaging, reduces the impact of market volatility on your overall returns.

6. Rebalance: Periodically review and rebalance your portfolio to maintain your desired asset allocation. Market fluctuations can cause your portfolio to drift from its original allocation.
By effectively managing risk and diversifying your investments, you can create a more resilient portfolio that is better equipped to withstand market volatility and achieve your financial goals over the long term. Remember that risk and return are interconnected, so finding the right balance for your individual situation is key.

Chapter 3: Building a Solid Financial Future

Setting Clear Financial Goals

Setting clear financial goals is a crucial step toward achieving your desired financial future. Well-defined goals provide direction, motivation, and a roadmap for your financial decisions. Here's how to set clear financial goals:

1. Define Your Goals:
Identify both short-term and long-term financial objectives. Short-term goals might include saving for a vacation or paying off credit card debt, while long-term goals could involve retirement, buying a home, or funding education.

2. Make Your Goals Specific and Measurable:
Clearly define your goals with specific details. For instance, instead of saying "save for retirement," specify the amount you want to have saved by a certain age.

3. Set a Timeline:

Establish a target date for achieving each goal. Having a timeline creates a sense of urgency and helps you allocate resources appropriately.

4. Determine the Costs:
Estimate the financial requirements for each goal. Break down the costs and consider factors like inflation and potential investment growth.

5. Prioritize Your Goals:
Rank your goals in order of importance. Decide which goals are most urgent and which can be pursued once others are achieved.

6. Align with Your Values:
Ensure your goals align with your values and aspirations. Your financial decisions should reflect what truly matters to you.

7. Break Down Goals:
Divide larger goals into smaller, manageable milestones. This makes them less

overwhelming and allows you to track progress more effectively.

8. Be Realistic:
Set goals that are achievable based on your current financial situation. Unrealistic goals can lead to frustration and derail your efforts.

9. Consider Financial Categories:
Categorize your goals into areas like savings, investments, debt reduction, and lifestyle expenses. This helps you organize your financial priorities.

10. Create an Action Plan:
Outline the steps you need to take to reach each goal. Determine how much you need to save or invest regularly, and identify any adjustments you might need to make to your spending habits.

11. Review and Adjust:

Regularly review your goals and progress. As your circumstances change, adjust your goals and strategies accordingly.

12. Stay Motivated:
Visualize the benefits of achieving your goals. Celebrate milestones along the way and stay motivated by reminding yourself of the positive impact your efforts will have on your life.

Setting clear financial goals provides a sense of purpose and direction, helping you make informed financial decisions that align with your aspirations. Regularly revisit your goals, celebrate achievements, and adapt your strategies as needed to ensure you're on track to realize your financial dreams.

Strategies for Debt Management

Effective debt management is crucial for achieving financial stability and working toward your long-term goals. Here are strategies to help you manage your debt more successfully:

1. Create a Comprehensive Debt List:
Compile a list of all your debts, including credit card balances, student loans, mortgages, and any other outstanding loans. Note the interest rates and minimum payments for each.

2. Prioritize High-Interest Debt:
Focus on paying off high-interest debts first. Allocate extra funds toward these debts while making minimum payments on lower-interest loans.

3. Develop a Budget:
Create a detailed budget that outlines your income and expenses. Allocate a portion of your budget to debt repayment while ensuring you cover essential expenses.

4. Snowball or Avalanche Method:
Choose a debt repayment strategy that suits your preferences. The snowball method involves paying off the smallest debt first, while the avalanche method targets the debt with the highest interest rate.

5. Consolidate Debt:
Consider consolidating multiple high-interest debts into a single lower-interest loan. This can simplify payments and reduce interest costs.

6. Negotiate Lower Interest Rates:
Contact your creditors to negotiate lower interest rates. A lower rate can significantly reduce the total interest you pay over time.

7. Refinance Loans:
Explore options to refinance high-interest loans, such as student loans or mortgages, to secure a lower interest rate and potentially lower monthly payments.

8. Avoid Taking on New Debt:
Refrain from accumulating new debt while focusing on paying off existing ones. Stick to your budget and avoid unnecessary purchases.

9. Use Windfalls Wisely:
Use unexpected windfalls, such as tax refunds or bonuses, to make extra payments toward your debts. This can accelerate your debt payoff journey.

10. Build an Emergency Fund:
Having an emergency fund can prevent you from relying on credit cards or loans for unexpected expenses, helping you avoid additional debt.

11. Seek Professional Help:
If your debt situation feels overwhelming, consider seeking help from a credit counseling agency or financial advisor. They can provide guidance and assistance in creating a debt management plan.

12. Monitor Your Progress:
Regularly track your debt repayment progress. Celebrate each milestone and use your progress as motivation to continue.

13. Practice Patience:

Debt management is a journey that takes time and discipline. Stay committed to your plan and be patient as you work toward becoming debt-free.

By implementing these strategies and staying committed to your debt management plan, you can take control of your financial situation, reduce debt stress, and pave the way for a more secure financial future.

Creating an Effective Emergency Fund

Creating an effective emergency fund is an essential step toward achieving financial security and peace of mind. An emergency fund provides a safety net to cover unexpected expenses or financial challenges. Here's how to create and manage an emergency fund:

1. Determine Your Target Amount:

Calculate how much you need in your emergency fund. A common guideline is to aim for three to six months' worth of living expenses. Adjust this based on your individual circumstances, such as job stability, family size, and health.

2. Start Small and Be Consistent:
If the thought of saving a large amount is daunting, start with a small goal and gradually increase it over time. Consistency is key – set up automatic transfers to your emergency fund each month.

3. Open a Dedicated Account:
Create a separate savings account specifically for your emergency fund. This separation makes it less tempting to dip into the fund for non-emergencies.

4. Prioritize Fund Growth:
Focus on building your emergency fund before aggressively investing or paying off low-interest debts. Your emergency fund serves as a financial buffer and should be easily accessible.

5. Save Windfalls and Bonuses:
Direct unexpected windfalls, such as tax refunds or work bonuses, into your emergency fund. This can help you reach your goal more quickly.

6. Cut Unnecessary Expenses:
Review your budget and identify areas where you can cut back on discretionary spending. Redirect the money you save toward your emergency fund.

7. Set Milestones:
Break down your emergency fund goal into smaller milestones. Celebrate each milestone you reach to stay motivated.

8. Avoid Temptation:
Only use your emergency fund for genuine emergencies, such as medical expenses, car repairs, or unexpected job loss. Avoid using it for non-urgent purchases.

9. Replenish After Use:
If you need to use your emergency fund, make a plan to replenish it as soon as possible to maintain its effectiveness.

10. Review and Adjust:
Regularly review your emergency fund to ensure it aligns with your current circumstances. Adjust the target amount if your financial situation changes.

11. Keep it Liquid:
Emergency funds should be easily accessible. Consider a high-yield savings account or a money market account that offers modest interest while allowing quick access to funds.
12. Protect Against Inflation:
Keep in mind that the cost of living may increase over time. Periodically review your emergency fund goal to account for inflation.

An effective emergency fund provides a financial cushion that can help you navigate unexpected challenges without derailing your financial progress. It's an important tool for building financial resilience and achieving your long-term goals. Start building your emergency fund today, and watch your financial security grow.

Chapter 4: The Psychology of Money

Overcoming Financial Anxiety

Overcoming financial anxiety is essential for maintaining your mental well-being and making sound financial decisions. Here are some strategies to help you manage and alleviate financial anxiety:

1. Face Your Fears:
Acknowledge your financial concerns and fears. Avoiding them can intensify anxiety. Confronting your fears allows you to address them head-on and develop a plan.

2. Educate Yourself:
Increase your financial literacy by learning about budgeting, investing, debt management, and other financial topics. Knowledge can empower you and reduce feelings of uncertainty.

3. Create a Budget:

Develop a comprehensive budget that tracks your income and expenses. Having a clear understanding of your financial situation can alleviate anxiety about where your money is going.

4. Break It Down:
If your financial situation feels overwhelming, break it down into manageable steps. Tackling one aspect at a time can make the process more manageable.

5. Seek Professional Help:
Consider consulting a financial advisor or a credit counselor. They can provide expert guidance and help you create a realistic financial plan.

6. Focus on What You Can Control:
Identify factors within your control and take action on them. This can help you feel more empowered and reduce feelings of helplessness.

7. Practice Mindfulness:

Engage in mindfulness techniques such as deep breathing, meditation, or yoga to manage stress and anxiety. Mindfulness can help you stay present and avoid ruminating on worst-case scenarios.

8. Set Realistic Goals:

Set achievable financial goals that are tailored to your situation. Unrealistic goals can lead to unnecessary stress and disappointment.

9. Limit Exposure to Negative Information:

Constant exposure to negative financial news can fuel anxiety. Stay informed, but avoid obsessively following every market fluctuation.

10. Develop Coping Strategies:

Identify healthy coping mechanisms for managing anxiety, such as exercise, spending time with loved ones, or engaging in hobbies you enjoy.

11. Celebrate Small Wins:
Acknowledge and celebrate your financial achievements, no matter how small. Building positive momentum can boost your confidence and reduce anxiety.

12. Practice Self-Compassion:
Be kind to yourself and avoid self-blame. Remember that financial challenges are common, and seeking help is a sign of strength.

13. Stay Connected:
Talk to friends, family, or a support group about your financial concerns. Sharing your feelings can provide emotional relief and help you realize you're not alone.

Remember that overcoming financial anxiety takes time. Be patient with yourself and consistently practice these strategies to gradually reduce anxiety and improve your financial well-being. If your anxiety becomes overwhelming, consider seeking professional help from a therapist or counselor.

Developing a Healthy Relationship with Money

Developing a healthy relationship with money is essential for your overall well-being and financial success. Here are key principles and practices to foster a positive and balanced relationship with money:

1. Understand Your Beliefs and Attitudes: Reflect on your beliefs and attitudes about money. Identify any negative thought patterns or inherited money messages that may be influencing your relationship with money.

2. Practice Gratitude:
Cultivate a sense of gratitude for what you have, rather than focusing solely on what you lack. Gratitude can shift your perspective and help you appreciate the value of your resources.

3. Define Your Values:
Clarify your core values and priorities in life. Align your financial decisions with these

values, ensuring that your money is being spent in ways that truly matter to you.

4. Set Boundaries:
Establish clear boundaries around your spending and financial decisions. Learn to say no to impulse purchases that don't align with your goals.

5. Practice Mindfulness:
Be present and mindful when making financial choices. Consider the consequences of your decisions and how they fit into your overall financial plan.

6. Focus on Financial Wellness:
View money as a tool for achieving overall wellness. This includes physical, emotional, and mental well-being, as well as financial security.

7. Avoid Comparisons:
Avoid comparing your financial situation to others. Everyone's journey is unique, and focusing on comparisons can lead to dissatisfaction and anxiety.

8. Embrace Simplicity:
Adopt a more minimalist approach to spending. Simplifying your lifestyle can reduce financial stress and increase your sense of contentment.

9. Plan and Budget:
Create a realistic financial plan and budget that aligns with your goals and values. Having a clear roadmap can reduce financial uncertainty and anxiety.

10. Practice Delayed Gratification:
Learn to delay instant gratification for greater long-term rewards. This can help you make more thoughtful and intentional financial decisions.

11. Seek Balance:
Strive for balance between spending, saving, and investing. Avoid extremes of excessive frugality or overspending.

12. Educate Yourself:
Continuously educate yourself about personal finance. Knowledge empowers you to make informed decisions and builds confidence in your financial choices.

13. Separate Self-Worth from Money:
Remember that your self-worth is not defined by your financial status. Your value as a person is separate from your financial achievements.

14. Celebrate Achievements:
Acknowledge and celebrate your financial successes, no matter how small. This positive reinforcement encourages responsible financial behavior.
Developing a healthy relationship with money takes time and self-awareness. Be patient with yourself and commit to making positive changes. By aligning your financial decisions with your values, practicing mindfulness, and cultivating gratitude, you can create a balanced and fulfilling relationship with money.

Behavioral Biases and their Impact on Financial Decisions

Behavioral biases are cognitive and emotional tendencies that can lead individuals to make irrational or suboptimal decisions. These biases can significantly impact financial decisions and lead to poor outcomes. Here are some common behavioral biases and their impact on financial choices:

1. Confirmation Bias:
Impact: People tend to seek out information that confirms their existing beliefs while ignoring or downplaying contradictory information.
Financial Impact: Investors may overlook warning signs about an investment they're emotionally attached to, leading to losses.

2. Overconfidence Bias:
Impact: Individuals tend to overestimate their abilities and knowledge, leading them to take on more risk than they should.

Financial Impact: Overconfident investors might trade excessively or make risky investments, resulting in losses.

3. Loss Aversion:

Impact: People feel the pain of losses more intensely than the pleasure of gains, causing them to avoid actions that might lead to losses.

Financial Impact: Investors may hold onto losing investments for too long, missing out on better opportunities.

4. Anchoring Bias:

Impact: People rely heavily on the first piece of information they receive (the anchor) when making decisions, even if it's irrelevant.

Financial Impact: Anchoring can lead investors to make decisions based on outdated or irrelevant information, affecting portfolio allocation.

5. Herd Mentality:

Impact: Individuals tend to follow the actions of a larger group, often leading to the adoption of trends without critical evaluation.
Financial Impact: Herd behavior can contribute to asset bubbles and market volatility as investors rush to buy or sell based on group sentiment.

6. Mental Accounting:
Impact: People compartmentalize their money into different mental accounts, treating different funds differently even if they have the same purpose.
Financial Impact: Mental accounting can lead to suboptimal spending and saving decisions, such as overspending from one account while neglecting another.

7. Sunk Cost Fallacy:
Impact: Individuals continue to invest resources (time, money, effort) into a decision based on past investment, even if the future benefits are low.

Financial Impact: People may hold onto losing investments simply because they've already put money into them, leading to further losses.

8. Availability Heuristic:
Impact: People rely on easily recalled information, often from recent events, to make judgments and decisions.
Financial Impact: Investors might make decisions based on recent market trends or news without considering the long-term implications.

9. Gambler's Fallacy:
Impact: Individuals believe that past random events influence future probabilities, leading to incorrect predictions.
Financial Impact: Investors may make decisions based on false assumptions about market patterns or trends.

10. Endowment Effect:
Impact: People tend to assign higher value to things they own compared to similar things they don't own.

Financial Impact: The endowment effect can lead to reluctance to sell investments at fair market value, causing missed opportunities.

Being aware of these biases and actively working to mitigate their effects can help you make more rational and informed financial decisions.

Chapter 5: Entrepreneurship and Wealth Creation

Navigating the World of Entrepreneurship

Navigating the world of entrepreneurship can be both exciting and challenging. Here are some key steps and considerations to help you embark on your entrepreneurial journey:

1. Idea Generation and Validation:
- Identify a business idea that solves a problem or fulfills a need in the market.
- Conduct thorough market research to validate your idea and understand your target audience.

2. Business Planning:
- Develop a comprehensive business plan outlining your goals, target market, value proposition, revenue model, and operational strategies.
- Define your business structure (sole proprietorship, partnership, LLC, corporation) and legal requirements.

3. Funding and Financing:
- Determine how much capital you need to start and operate your business.
- Explore funding options such as personal savings, loans, investors, crowdfunding, or angel investors.

4. Branding and Marketing:
- Create a strong brand identity, including a logo, website, and marketing materials.
- Develop a marketing strategy to reach and engage your target audience through social media, content marketing, advertising, and networking.

5. Product or Service Development:

- Design and develop your product or service, focusing on quality, usability, and customer satisfaction.
- Test your product/service with a small group of customers to gather feedback and make improvements.

6. Legal and Regulatory Compliance:
- Register your business name, obtain necessary licenses, permits, and certifications.
- Comply with local, state, and federal regulations related to taxes, employment, and operations.

7. Operations and Logistics:
- Set up efficient and streamlined operational processes for production, distribution, customer service, and order fulfillment.

8. Financial Management:
- Establish a budget and financial projections to track expenses, revenue, and profitability.
- Implement proper accounting practices and consider hiring a professional if needed.

9. Team Building:

- Hire employees or collaborate with freelancers/contractors as your business grows.
- Build a team with complementary skills to support different aspects of your business.

10. Adaptability and Learning:
- Embrace a growth mindset and be prepared to pivot or adapt your business model based on market feedback and changing circumstances.
- Continuously educate yourself about entrepreneurship, industry trends, and new technologies.

11. Networking and Relationships:
- Build a strong network of mentors, advisors, peers, and potential customers.
- Attend industry events, conferences, and workshops to expand your connections and knowledge.

12. Resilience and Perseverance:
- Entrepreneurship can be challenging, so cultivate resilience and the ability to overcome setbacks and failures.

13. Work-Life Balance:
- Strive to maintain a healthy work-life balance to avoid burnout and maintain your overall well-being.

Remember that entrepreneurship is a journey with ups and downs. Be prepared to learn from your experiences and continuously adapt to the evolving business landscape. Seek guidance, stay persistent, and remain focused on your vision to increase your chances of building a successful and fulfilling entrepreneurial venture.

Scaling a Business for Profitability

Scaling a business for profitability involves strategically expanding your operations to increase revenue while managing costs effectively. Here are key steps to help you scale your business successfully:

1. Solidify Your Foundation:

- Ensure your core business model is well-established and profitable before scaling. Address any operational inefficiencies or challenges.

2. Market Research:
- Conduct thorough market research to identify new growth opportunities, target markets, and customer segments.

3. Develop a Scalable Strategy:
- Create a detailed plan outlining how you will expand your business while maintaining quality and efficiency.
- Consider diversifying your product or service offerings, entering new markets, or expanding your distribution channels.

4. Strengthen Operations:
- Streamline and optimize your operational processes to handle increased demand efficiently.
- Invest in technology and automation to improve productivity and reduce manual tasks.

5. Build a Strong Team:
- Hire talented and skilled individuals to support your expansion. Delegate responsibilities and empower your team members.

6. Marketing and Branding:
- Develop a robust marketing strategy to increase brand awareness and attract new customers.
- Utilize digital marketing, social media, and content marketing to reach a broader audience.

7. Customer Experience:
- Maintain a strong focus on delivering excellent customer service to retain existing customers and attract new ones through positive word-of-mouth.

8. Financial Management:
- Monitor your finances closely and ensure you have the necessary capital to support expansion.
- Implement effective budgeting, financial forecasting, and cash flow management.

9. Strategic Partnerships:
- Collaborate with other businesses or strategic partners to leverage their resources and reach a wider audience.

10. Test and Iterate:
- Test your scaled strategies on a smaller scale before fully implementing them. Gather feedback and make necessary adjustments.

11. Measure Key Metrics:
- Identify key performance indicators (KPIs) related to your growth goals, such as customer acquisition cost, customer lifetime value, and revenue growth.

12. Monitor Competition:
- Stay informed about your competitors' activities and adjust your strategies accordingly to maintain a competitive edge.

13. Stay Customer-Centric:
- Keep the customer's needs and preferences at the forefront of your scaling efforts.

Continuously seek feedback and adapt your offerings accordingly.

14. Manage Risks:
- Identify potential risks associated with scaling, such as increased costs, supply chain disruptions, or changes in market demand. Develop contingency plans to mitigate these risks.

15. Iterate and Learn:
- Scaling is an ongoing process. Continuously monitor results, gather data, and iterate on your strategies to optimize growth and profitability.

Remember that scaling a business requires careful planning, resources, and dedication. It's important to strike a balance between growth and maintaining the quality and values that made your business successful in the first place. By following these steps and remaining adaptable, you can successfully scale your business for increased profitability.

Innovations in the Digital Age

The digital age has brought about numerous innovations that have transformed the way we live, work, and interact. Here are some key innovations that have emerged in the digital age:

1. Internet and Connectivity:
The widespread availability of the internet has revolutionized communication, information sharing, and access to knowledge on a global scale. High-speed internet and wireless connectivity have enabled seamless communication and collaboration.

2. Mobile Technology:
The advent of smartphones and mobile apps has empowered individuals to access information, services, and entertainment from anywhere at any time. Mobile technology has also facilitated the rise of mobile banking, e-commerce, and social networking.

3. Cloud Computing:
Cloud computing allows users to store and access data, applications, and services

remotely over the internet. It has transformed how businesses manage their IT infrastructure, enabling scalability and cost-efficiency.

4. Artificial Intelligence (AI) and Machine Learning:

AI and machine learning technologies have enabled computers to perform tasks that typically require human intelligence, such as language processing, image recognition, and data analysis. They have applications in various industries, including healthcare, finance, and manufacturing.

5. Internet of Things (IoT):

IoT refers to the network of interconnected devices and objects that can communicate and exchange data. IoT technology has enabled smart homes, wearable devices, and improved supply chain management.

6. Blockchain Technology:

Blockchain is a distributed and decentralized digital ledger that ensures transparency, security, and immutability of transactions. It has applications in cryptocurrency, supply chain management, and digital identity verification.

7. Virtual and Augmented Reality (VR/AR):
VR and AR technologies offer immersive and interactive experiences. They are used in gaming, education, training, and even virtual tours of real estate properties.

8. Big Data Analytics:
The availability of vast amounts of data has led to the development of sophisticated data analytics tools. Big data analytics helps businesses make informed decisions, understand consumer behavior, and optimize operations.

9. E-commerce and Online Marketplaces:
E-commerce platforms have revolutionized retail, allowing businesses to sell products and services online. Online marketplaces like Amazon and Alibaba have transformed how consumers shop and businesses operate.

10. Digital Payments and Cryptocurrencies:

Digital payment systems and cryptocurrencies have disrupted traditional financial transactions. They offer faster, more secure, and borderless ways to transfer money.

11. Renewable Energy Technologies:
Digital innovations have contributed to the advancement of renewable energy sources, such as solar and wind power. Smart grids and energy management systems enhance the efficiency and reliability of energy distribution.

12. Telemedicine and Remote Work Solutions:
Digital tools have enabled remote healthcare services (telemedicine) and remote work capabilities. This became even more significant during the COVID-19 pandemic.

These innovations continue to evolve and shape our world, driving economic growth, improving efficiency, and enhancing our quality of life. As technology continues to advance, we can expect further transformative changes in various sectors and aspects of our lives.

Chapter 6: Real Estate Riches

Real Estate Investment Strategies

Real estate investment offers various strategies for investors to generate income, build wealth, and diversify their portfolios. Here are some common real estate investment strategies:

1. Buy and Hold:
Investors purchase properties with the intention of holding them for the long term, generating rental income and benefiting from potential appreciation in property value.

2. Flipping:
Investors buy distressed properties, renovate or improve them, and then sell quickly for a profit. This strategy requires a good understanding of market trends and property valuation.

3. Rental Properties:

Investors acquire properties and rent them out to tenants. Rental income provides a steady cash flow, and properties can appreciate over time.

4. Commercial Real Estate:
Investing in commercial properties, such as office buildings, retail spaces, and warehouses, offers higher potential returns but often requires larger upfront investments.

5. Real Estate Investment Trusts (REITs):
REITs are companies that own or finance income-generating real estate. Investors can buy shares in a publicly-traded REIT, allowing them to invest in real estate without directly owning properties.

6. Real Estate Crowdfunding:
Investors pool their funds through online platforms to invest in specific real estate projects, such as developments or renovations. This allows for diversification with smaller investment amounts.

7. Wholesaling:

Investors identify distressed properties, put them under contract at a discounted price, and then assign the contract to another buyer for a fee.

8. Lease Options:
Investors enter into a lease agreement with the option to purchase the property at a predetermined price at a later date. This strategy can provide potential profit while controlling the property.

9. House Hacking:
Investors live in one unit of a multifamily property while renting out the other units. This strategy helps cover living expenses and can lead to mortgage-free living.

10. Short-Term Rentals:
Investors list properties on platforms like Airbnb for short-term stays, often generating higher rental income compared to traditional long-term rentals.

11. Tax Lien Investing:
Investors purchase tax liens on properties with delinquent property taxes. If the property owner fails to pay, the investor can potentially acquire the property.

12. Private Lending:
Investors provide loans to real estate developers or flippers in exchange for interest payments. This strategy requires careful due diligence and risk assessment.

13. International Real Estate:
Investing in properties abroad can offer diversification and potential for strong returns, but it also involves unique challenges and considerations.

Each strategy comes with its own risks, rewards, and requirements. Before diving into real estate investing, it's important to research, educate yourself, and consider factors such as market conditions, location, financing options, and your risk tolerance. Consulting with real estate professionals and financial advisors can help you make informed investment decisions.

Maximizing Rental Income

Maximizing rental income from your investment properties requires strategic planning, effective management, and a focus on tenant satisfaction. Here are some tips to help you maximize rental income:

1. Competitive Rent Pricing:
Conduct market research to determine the appropriate rent for your property based on its location, size, features, and comparable properties in the area. Pricing your rent competitively can attract tenants and reduce vacancy periods.

2. Regular Maintenance and Upgrades:
Maintain the property in good condition to attract quality tenants and justify higher rent. Regularly inspect and address maintenance issues promptly. Consider making upgrades that add value and appeal to tenants, such as

modern appliances, updated fixtures, or
energy-efficient features.

3. Add Value with Amenities:
Offer amenities that stand out and justify
higher rent, such as laundry facilities, parking
spaces, fitness centers, or pet-friendly
features. These amenities can attract tenants
willing to pay more for added convenience
and comfort.

4. Improve Curb Appeal:
Enhance the property's curb appeal with
landscaping, exterior improvements, and a
well-maintained appearance. A visually
appealing property can attract higher-quality
tenants and command higher rent.

5. Efficient Property Management:
Effective property management can lead to
higher tenant satisfaction and longer lease
terms. Respond promptly to tenant inquiries,
address concerns, and ensure a smooth rental
experience.

6. Long-Term Leases:

Consider offering longer lease terms to tenants who are willing to commit to renting for an extended period. Longer leases provide stability and reduce turnover costs.

7. Screen Tenants Thoroughly:
Select tenants carefully by conducting thorough background checks, credit screenings, and rental history verification. Quality tenants are more likely to pay higher rent and take good care of the property.

8. Rent Increases:
Regularly review market conditions and consider implementing rent increases when justified by market trends and property improvements. Be mindful of local rent control regulations.

9. Offer Furnished Rentals:
Depending on the market and target tenant demographic, offering furnished rentals can allow you to charge a premium rent and attract tenants seeking convenience.

10. Strategic Marketing:

Effectively market your property to reach a wider audience. Use high-quality photos, detailed property descriptions, and online platforms to showcase the property's features and benefits.

11. Tenant Retention:
Prioritize tenant satisfaction to encourage lease renewals. Address tenant concerns, offer incentives for renewing leases, and create a positive rental experience.

12. Consider Short-Term Rentals:
If the local regulations and market conditions permit, you may explore the option of short-term rentals, which can yield higher rental income, especially in popular tourist areas.

By implementing these strategies and continuously assessing market trends and tenant preferences, you can optimize your rental income and enhance the financial performance of your investment properties.

Flipping Properties for Profit

Flipping properties for profit involves buying distressed or undervalued properties, making strategic improvements, and selling them quickly for a higher price. Here's a step-by-step guide to successfully flip properties for profit:

1. Research and Analysis:
- Identify your target market and location. Research local real estate trends, property values, and market demand.
- Analyze potential properties to determine their current value, repair costs, and potential resale value.

2. Financing and Budgeting:
- Secure financing through savings, loans, or private investors. Set a budget that includes the purchase price, renovation costs, and other expenses.

3. Property Acquisition:
- Search for distressed properties, foreclosures, or properties in need of renovation. Negotiate a favorable purchase price.

- Perform due diligence to uncover any
potential issues or liabilities with the
property.

4. Renovation and Improvement:
- Develop a detailed renovation plan. Focus
on cost-effective improvements that add
value, such as kitchen and bathroom
upgrades, flooring, paint, and landscaping.
- Obtain necessary permits and hire qualified
contractors or manage the renovations
yourself if you have the skills.

5. Time Management:
- Plan a realistic timeline for the renovation
process. Time is of the essence in property
flipping to minimize holding costs.

6. Marketing and Selling:
- Stage the property to showcase its best
features. Use high-quality photos for
marketing materials.
- Price the property competitively based on its
renovated condition and comparable
properties in the area.

- List the property on real estate websites, work with a real estate agent, and use other marketing channels to attract potential buyers.

7. Negotiation and Closing:
- Respond promptly to offers from interested buyers. Negotiate terms that align with your profit goals.
- Complete all necessary paperwork and work with a real estate attorney or agent to ensure a smooth closing process.

8. Calculate Costs and Profit:
- Deduct all expenses, including acquisition costs, renovation costs, holding costs (property taxes, utilities, insurance), and selling costs (agent commissions, closing costs).
- Calculate your estimated profit to ensure the flip is financially viable.

9. Risk Management:
- Be prepared for unexpected challenges, such as renovation delays, budget overruns, or changes in market conditions.

- Have a backup plan in case the property doesn't sell as quickly as anticipated.

10. Continuous Learning:
- Learn from each property flip experience. Assess what worked well and what could be improved for future flips.

Remember, property flipping involves financial risk and requires careful planning, research, and execution. While successful flips can yield substantial profits, there's no guarantee of success in every market condition. Consult with experienced real estate professionals, contractors, and financial advisors to make informed decisions and maximize your chances of a successful property flip.

Chapter 7: Retirement Planning and Wealth Preservation

Exploring Retirement Account Options

Exploring retirement account options is an important step in planning for your financial future. Different types of retirement accounts offer various tax advantages and features. Here are some common retirement account options to consider:

1. 401(k) Plans:
- Employer-sponsored retirement plans offered by private companies.
- Contributions are made pre-tax, reducing your taxable income.
- Employers may match a portion of your contributions.
- Withdrawals are generally taxed as ordinary income in retirement.

2. Traditional IRAs (Individual Retirement Accounts):
- Personal retirement accounts with tax-deductible contributions, subject to income limits.
- Earnings grow tax-deferred, and withdrawals in retirement are taxed as ordinary income.
- You can contribute even if you don't have an employer-sponsored plan.

3. Roth IRAs:
- Similar to traditional IRAs, but contributions are made with after-tax dollars.
- Earnings grow tax-free, and qualified withdrawals in retirement are also tax-free.

- Income limits apply for Roth IRA
contributions.

4. SEP IRAs (Simplified Employee Pension
IRAs):
- Designed for self-employed individuals and
small business owners.
- Contributions are tax-deductible and can be
higher than traditional IRAs.
- Employer contributions are made on behalf
of eligible employees.

5. SIMPLE IRAs (Savings Incentive Match
Plan for Employees):
- Designed for small businesses with fewer
than 100 employees.
- Employees and employers make
contributions, with potential employer
matching.
- Lower administrative costs compared to
401(k) plans.

6. Solo 401(k) (Individual 401(k)):
- Designed for self-employed individuals and
small business owners without employees.

- Similar to traditional 401(k) plans, with the option for employer and employee contributions.

7. 403(b) Plans:
- Retirement plans for employees of public schools, tax-exempt organizations, and certain ministers.
- Similar to 401(k) plans but with specific regulations for qualifying employers.

8. Governmental 457 Plans:
- Offered by state and local governments and certain tax-exempt organizations.
- Similar to 401(k) plans but with unique features and withdrawal options.

9. Defined Benefit Plans (Pensions):
- Offered by some employers, especially government entities.
- Provide a specific monthly benefit in retirement based on factors like salary and years of service.

10. Health Savings Accounts (HSAs):

- Not specifically retirement accounts, but HSAs can be used for medical expenses in retirement.
- Contributions are tax-deductible, earnings grow tax-free, and withdrawals for qualified medical expenses are tax-free.

It's important to consider factors such as your employment status, income level, and retirement goals when choosing the right retirement account(s) for you. Consulting with a financial advisor can help you make informed decisions and create a retirement strategy that aligns with your financial objectives.

Estate Planning and Inheritance Management

Estate planning and inheritance management are crucial aspects of financial planning that involve arranging your affairs to ensure your assets are distributed according to your wishes and to minimize the impact of taxes and legal complications. Here are key steps and considerations for effective estate planning and inheritance management:

1. Create a Will:
- A will is a legal document that outlines how you want your assets to be distributed after your death.
- Designate an executor to carry out the terms of your will and manage your estate.

2. Establish a Living Trust:
- A living trust allows you to transfer assets to a trust during your lifetime, which can help avoid probate and provide greater control over asset distribution.

3. Designate Beneficiaries:
- Ensure that your retirement accounts, life insurance policies, and other financial assets have designated beneficiaries. These assets can pass directly to beneficiaries without going through probate.

4. Power of Attorney:
- Assign a trusted individual as your power of attorney to make financial and medical

decisions on your behalf if you become incapacitated.

5. Health Care Proxy:
- Appoint someone to make medical decisions for you if you're unable to do so.

6. Guardianship for Minor Children:
- If you have minor children, specify a guardian who will take care of them in the event of your death.

7. Charitable Giving:
- If you want to leave a portion of your estate to charitable organizations, consider establishing charitable trusts or bequests in your will.

8. Minimize Estate Taxes:
- Understand the estate tax laws in your jurisdiction and explore strategies to minimize potential estate taxes, such as gifting, establishing irrevocable trusts, or

using the unified federal gift and estate tax exemption.

9. Review and Update:
- Regularly review and update your estate plan to reflect changes in your financial situation, family structure, and goals.

10. Communicate with Family:
- Openly discuss your estate plan with your family members to ensure they understand your wishes and intentions.

11. Consider Long-Term Care:
- Plan for the possibility of needing long-term care and explore options for funding it, such as long-term care insurance.

12. Consult Legal and Financial Professionals:
- Work with an experienced estate planning attorney and financial advisor to ensure your estate plan aligns with your objectives and complies with legal requirements.

13. Gather Important Documents:
- Organize and store important documents, such as your will, trust documents, insurance policies, and financial account information in a secure location.

14. Plan for Digital Assets:
- Include provisions for your digital assets, such as online accounts, social media profiles, and digital files.

Effective estate planning and inheritance management can provide peace of mind and ensure that your loved ones are taken care of according to your wishes. Start the process early, and regularly review and update your plan to adapt to changing circumstances.

Strategies for Long-Term Wealth Preservation

Preserving long-term wealth requires careful planning, disciplined financial strategies, and a focus on protecting and growing your assets over time. Here are some strategies for long-term wealth preservation:

1. Diversify Your Investments:
Spread your investments across different asset classes, industries, and geographic regions. Diversification can help reduce risk and protect your wealth from fluctuations in any one area.

2. Invest for the Long Term:
Adopt a long-term investment approach that aligns with your financial goals. Avoid making impulsive decisions based on short-term market fluctuations.

3. Tax Efficiency:
Minimize your tax liability by utilizing tax-efficient investment accounts and strategies. Consider tax-advantaged accounts like IRAs, 401(k)s, and HSAs, and be mindful of capital gains taxes.

4. Asset Protection:
Protect your assets from potential lawsuits and creditors by utilizing legal structures such

as trusts, limited liability companies (LLCs), and family limited partnerships (FLPs).

5. Estate Planning:
Create a comprehensive estate plan that includes a will, trusts, and other legal documents to ensure your assets are distributed according to your wishes and to minimize estate taxes.

6. Regular Rebalancing:
Periodically review and rebalance your investment portfolio to maintain your desired asset allocation. Rebalancing can help you manage risk and maintain a diversified portfolio.

7. Risk Management:
Obtain adequate insurance coverage, including health, life, home, and liability insurance, to protect your assets from unexpected events.

8. Avoid Excessive Debt:
Use debt judiciously and avoid taking on excessive debt that could strain your financial

situation. Pay off high-interest debt as a priority.

9. Continual Learning:
Stay informed about financial markets, investment strategies, and tax regulations. Continuously educate yourself to make informed decisions.

10. Maintain Liquidity:
Keep a portion of your wealth in liquid assets such as cash, money market accounts, or short-term investments. This provides a financial cushion for emergencies and opportunities.

11. Manage Lifestyle Inflation:
Avoid excessive spending increases as your wealth grows. Maintain a reasonable and sustainable lifestyle to ensure your assets last.

12. Professional Guidance:
Work with experienced financial advisors, tax professionals, and estate planning attorneys

who can provide personalized guidance based on your financial goals and circumstances.

13. Philanthropy and Charitable Giving:
Consider establishing charitable foundations, donor-advised funds, or charitable trusts as part of your wealth preservation strategy. Charitable giving can have tax benefits and help leave a lasting legacy.

14. Review and Update:
Regularly review your financial plan and investment strategy to ensure they remain aligned with your goals and adapt to changes in your life, the economy, and the financial landscape.

Remember that long-term wealth preservation requires discipline, patience, and a commitment to your financial well-being. By implementing these strategies and maintaining a prudent approach, you can work towards preserving your wealth for your own future and for generations to come.

Chapter 8: Achieving Financial Freedom

Building Multiple Streams of Income

Building multiple streams of income is a smart strategy to increase financial stability, flexibility, and wealth accumulation. Here are some ways to diversify your income sources:

1. Active Income:
- Your primary job or profession provides the bulk of your income. Consider ways to increase your earning potential, such as advancing in your career, taking on freelance work, or starting a side business.

2. Passive Income:
- Income generated with minimal ongoing effort or active involvement. Examples include rental income from real estate, dividends from investments, and royalties from intellectual property.

3. Investments:

- Invest in stocks, bonds, mutual funds, exchange-traded funds (ETFs), and other assets that generate capital gains, dividends, and interest over time.

4. Real Estate Investments:
- Owning rental properties or investing in real estate crowdfunding platforms can provide rental income and potential property value appreciation.

5. Dividend Stocks:
- Invest in dividend-paying stocks to receive regular dividend payments from companies.

6. Side Business or Freelancing:
- Start a side business or offer your skills as a freelancer or consultant. This can generate additional income while allowing you to pursue your passions.

7. Affiliate Marketing or E-Commerce:
- Earn commissions by promoting products or services through affiliate marketing

programs. Alternatively, start an e-commerce business by selling products online.

8. Peer-to-Peer Lending:
- Participate in peer-to-peer lending platforms, where you lend money to individuals or small businesses in exchange for interest payments.

9. Rental Income:
- Rent out a spare room on platforms like Airbnb or become a landlord by investing in residential or commercial real estate properties.

10. Online Courses or eBooks:
- Create and sell online courses or eBooks on platforms like Udemy or Amazon Kindle Direct Publishing.

11. Royalties and Licensing:
- If you have intellectual property, such as music, books, patents, or artwork, you can earn royalties from their use or licensing.

12. Create a YouTube Channel or Blog:

- Generate income through ads, sponsorships, and affiliate marketing by creating valuable content on platforms like YouTube or a personal blog.

13. Create a Mobile App:
- If you have programming skills, create a mobile app that solves a specific problem or provides value to users.

14. Network Marketing or Multi-Level Marketing (MLM):
- Participate in network marketing companies that allow you to earn commissions by selling products and recruiting others.

15. Retirement Accounts:
- Contribute to retirement accounts like IRAs and 401(k)s, which can grow over time and provide income in retirement.

Diversifying your income sources requires careful planning, dedication, and a willingness to learn. Start by identifying your strengths, interests, and opportunities that align with your financial goals. It's important to manage your time effectively and ensure that your multiple income streams are sustainable and compatible with your lifestyle. Remember to consult financial professionals for guidance and make informed decisions based on your unique circumstances.

Balancing Work and Life for Long-Term Success

Balancing work and life is essential for maintaining long-term success, well-being, and overall happiness. Here are some strategies to help you achieve a healthy work-life balance:

1. Set Clear Boundaries:
- Establish clear boundaries between work and personal life. Define specific work hours and stick to them as much as possible.

2. Prioritize Tasks:
- Prioritize tasks based on importance and urgency. Focus on high-priority tasks during

work hours and allocate time for personal activities.

3. Time Management:
- Use time management techniques such as the Pomodoro Technique or time blocking to stay focused and efficient during work hours.

4. Delegate and Outsource:
- Delegate tasks at work when possible, and consider outsourcing personal tasks that consume your time.

5. Learn to Say No:
- Politely decline additional work or commitments if they interfere with your work-life balance.

6. Schedule Breaks:
- Schedule regular breaks during your workday to recharge and avoid burnout. Use breaks to stretch, meditate, or take short walks.

7. Unplug:

- Set designated times to disconnect from work emails and notifications, allowing you to fully engage in personal activities.

8. Plan Personal Activities:
- Schedule personal activities and hobbies just like you would work tasks. This ensures you have dedicated time for relaxation and enjoyment.

9. Family and Social Time:
- Allocate quality time for family and friends. Engage in meaningful conversations and activities to strengthen relationships.

10. Practice Self-Care:
- Prioritize self-care activities such as exercise, meditation, healthy eating, and adequate sleep to maintain your physical and mental well-being.

11. Flexibility:
- Embrace flexibility in your work schedule when possible. This can help accommodate personal responsibilities and activities.

12. Learn to Disconnect:
- When you're not working, truly disconnect from work-related thoughts and stressors.

13. Communicate Openly:
- Communicate your boundaries and work-life balance needs to your colleagues, supervisors, and family members.

14. Set Long-Term Goals:
- Define your long-term career and personal goals. Striving for a balanced life is easier when you have a clear vision of what you want to achieve.

15. Regularly Reflect:
- Take time to reflect on your work-life balance. Make adjustments as needed to ensure you're achieving your desired equilibrium.

Remember, work-life balance is a dynamic process that may require adjustments over time. Regularly assess your priorities, evaluate your progress, and make conscious choices to maintain a healthy balance that supports your long-term success and overall well-being.

Strategies for Early Retirement

Achieving early retirement requires careful planning, disciplined saving, and strategic financial decisions. Here are some strategies to consider if you're aiming for early retirement:

1. Define Your Financial Goals:
- Determine your target retirement age and the lifestyle you want in retirement. Calculate how much money you'll need to cover your expenses.

2. Increase Savings Rate:
- Save a higher percentage of your income to accelerate your retirement savings. Aim to save at least 15-20% of your income or more if possible.

3. Minimize Debt:

- Prioritize paying off high-interest debt like credit cards and personal loans. Minimize mortgage and student loan debt as well.

4. Invest Wisely:
- Invest your savings in a diversified portfolio of stocks, bonds, and other assets to maximize growth potential over the long term.

5. Take Advantage of Retirement Accounts:
- Contribute to tax-advantaged retirement accounts like IRAs and 401(k)s to benefit from tax deductions and tax-deferred growth.

6. Consider Roth Accounts:
- Roth IRAs and Roth 401(k)s allow for tax-free withdrawals in retirement. Consider contributing to these accounts if you anticipate being in a higher tax bracket in the future.

7. Create Multiple Income Streams:
- Develop additional income streams, such as rental properties, side businesses, or passive

investments, to supplement your retirement savings.

8. Control Expenses:
- Track your expenses and identify areas where you can cut back. Focus on reducing discretionary spending to increase your savings rate.

9. Live Below Your Means:
- Avoid lifestyle inflation and live on less than your income allows. Allocate windfalls like bonuses and tax refunds to your retirement savings.

10. Downsizing and Relocating:
- Consider downsizing your home or relocating to a more affordable area to reduce housing costs in retirement.
11. Health Insurance:
- Plan for healthcare costs in retirement. Research health insurance options and consider purchasing long-term care insurance to mitigate potential expenses.

12. Delay Social Security Benefits:

- Delaying your Social Security benefits beyond the minimum age can increase your monthly payments.

13. Reassess Your Plan Regularly:
- Monitor your progress and adjust your retirement plan as needed based on changing circumstances, market conditions, and goals.

14. Seek Professional Advice:
- Consult with a financial advisor to create a comprehensive retirement plan tailored to your specific situation and goals.

15. Be Realistic:
- While early retirement is achievable, be realistic about the sacrifices and trade-offs required to reach your goal. Make informed decisions that align with your priorities.

Remember that early retirement requires disciplined saving, careful financial management, and a long-term perspective. It's important to strike a balance between enjoying life now and preparing for a secure and fulfilling retirement in the future.

Chapter 9: Navigating Economic Ups and Downs

Thriving in a Volatile Market

Thriving in a volatile market requires a combination of strategic planning, emotional resilience, and a focus on long-term goals. Here are some strategies to help you navigate and even thrive in a volatile market:

1. Diversify Your Portfolio:
- Diversification involves spreading your investments across different asset classes, sectors, and geographic regions. This can help reduce the impact of a downturn in any single area.

2. Stay Informed:

- Keep yourself updated on market trends, economic indicators, and global events that could impact your investments. Knowledge is key to making informed decisions.

3. Focus on the Long Term:
- Maintain a long-term perspective and avoid making impulsive decisions based on short-term market fluctuations.

4. Emergency Fund:
- Have an emergency fund in place to cover unexpected expenses or to provide a financial buffer during market downturns.

5. Risk Tolerance and Asset Allocation:
- Align your investment choices with your risk tolerance. Your asset allocation should be in line with your comfort level and long-term financial goals.

6. Dollar-Cost Averaging:

- Invest a fixed amount of money at regular intervals, regardless of market conditions. This strategy can help smooth out the impact of market volatility.

7. Rebalance Regularly:
- Periodically review and rebalance your portfolio to maintain your desired asset allocation. This ensures you're not overly exposed to a particular asset class.

8. Avoid Emotional Decision-Making:
- Don't let fear or greed drive your investment decisions. Emotional reactions can lead to impulsive actions that may not align with your long-term goals.

9. Focus on Quality:
- Invest in high-quality companies or assets with solid fundamentals and strong growth potential, even during market fluctuations.

10. Keep Costs Low:
- Minimize investment costs by choosing low-cost funds and avoiding frequent trading. High fees can erode your returns over time.

11. Have a Plan:
- Develop a comprehensive financial plan that outlines your goals, risk tolerance, and investment strategy. Stick to your plan even during market volatility.

12. Seek Professional Guidance:
- Consult with a financial advisor who can provide expert advice and help you stay on track with your financial goals.

13. Maintain Cash Reserves:
- Keep a portion of your investments in cash or cash-equivalents, which can provide stability and liquidity during market downturns.

14. Avoid Timing the Market:
- Trying to time the market by predicting when to buy or sell can be risky. Focus on your long-term investment strategy instead.

15. Learn from Past Downturns:
- Study how markets have historically recovered from downturns. This can provide perspective and help you stay patient during volatile times.

Remember that market volatility is a natural part of investing, and it's important to stay focused on your long-term financial goals. By following these strategies and maintaining a disciplined approach, you can position yourself to thrive even in the face of market fluctuations.

Adapting to Economic Changes

Adapting to economic changes is essential for maintaining financial stability and success. Economic conditions can fluctuate due to various factors, including market trends, technological advancements, geopolitical events, and macroeconomic shifts. Here are some strategies to help you adapt to economic changes:

1. Stay Informed:
- Keep yourself updated on economic news, market trends, and shifts in industry dynamics. Knowledge is key to making informed decisions.

2. Diversify Income Sources:
- Develop multiple streams of income to reduce reliance on a single source. This can provide stability during economic downturns.

3. Continuous Learning:
- Invest in your education and skill development. Acquiring new skills can enhance your employability and open up opportunities in changing industries.

4. Build a Strong Network:
- Cultivate professional relationships and networks that can provide support, insights, and potential opportunities during economic shifts.

5. Be Flexible and Adaptable:
- Be open to change and willing to pivot your career, business, or investment strategies based on evolving economic conditions.
6. Budget and Save:
- Maintain a budget and save for emergencies. Having a financial cushion can help you weather unexpected economic challenges.

7. Monitor Debt:
- Manage and reduce debt to ensure that financial obligations are manageable even during economic uncertainties.

8. Embrace Technology:
- Leverage technology to stay competitive and relevant in your field. Embracing digital tools can enhance efficiency and open up new avenues.

9. Focus on Value:
- Provide value to your clients, customers, or employers. Offering exceptional products or services can help you stand out regardless of economic conditions.

10. Assess Investments:
- Regularly review your investment portfolio to ensure it aligns with your financial goals and risk tolerance. Adjust your investments as needed based on economic trends.

11. Maintain Relationships:
- Nurture relationships with clients, customers, and colleagues. Strong relationships can lead to referrals and business opportunities during economic changes.

12. Plan for Retirement:
- Create a retirement plan that accounts for potential economic fluctuations. Consider diversifying retirement investments to manage risk.

13. Consider New Opportunities:
- Explore new industries or sectors that may be thriving during changing economic conditions. Be open to taking calculated risks.

14. Seek Professional Advice:

- Consult with financial advisors, career counselors, or business mentors who can provide guidance tailored to your situation.

15. Stay Positive and Resilient:
- Maintain a positive mindset and cultivate resilience. Challenges are opportunities for growth and innovation.

Adapting to economic changes requires a proactive and forward-thinking approach. By staying informed, being flexible, and taking strategic actions, you can navigate economic shifts and position yourself for long-term success.

Turning Crises into Opportunities

Turning crises into opportunities requires a combination of creativity, resilience, and strategic thinking. Here are some ways to transform challenges into positive outcomes:

1. Embrace a Growth Mindset:
- View crises as opportunities for growth and learning. Adopt a positive attitude that

focuses on finding solutions and adapting to change.

2. Identify Emerging Needs:
- Analyze the crisis to identify new needs or gaps in the market. Look for ways to address these needs with innovative products or services.

3. Pivot Your Business Model:
- Adapt your business model to align with changing market conditions. Explore new revenue streams, distribution channels, or target markets.

4. Innovate and Create:
- Channel your creativity to develop innovative solutions that solve problems arising from the crisis. Innovations can lead to new business opportunities.

5. Learn from Feedback:

- Listen to customer feedback and adapt your offerings based on their changing preferences and needs.

6. Build Strategic Partnerships:
- Collaborate with other businesses or organizations to leverage each other's strengths and resources. Partnerships can open up new avenues for growth.

7. Digital Transformation:
- Embrace technology to enhance your operations, reach customers online, and create digital products or services.

8. Focus on Efficiency:
- Optimize your processes to become more efficient and cost-effective. Streamlining operations can lead to increased profitability.

9. Seek Funding Opportunities:
- Explore funding options such as grants, loans, or investment to support new initiatives or expand your business.

10. Upskill and Reskill:

- Invest in your own skills and the skills of your team. Learning new skills can lead to career advancement and new business opportunities.

11. Expand Online Presence:
- Enhance your online presence through social media, e-commerce, and digital marketing. Online visibility can attract new customers and clients.

12. Provide Value:
- Offer value to your customers by providing solutions that help them navigate the crisis. This can build loyalty and trust.

13. Look for Underserved Markets:
- Identify markets or niches that may have been overlooked and tailor your offerings to meet their specific needs.

14. Focus on Sustainability:
- Consider how your business can contribute to a more sustainable future. Environmental and social considerations can create opportunities for differentiation.

15. Stay Agile:
- Remain flexible and adaptable to changing circumstances. Being agile allows you to seize opportunities quickly and pivot as needed.

Chapter 10: Inspiring Success Stories

Interviews with Self-Made Millionaires and Billionaires

Interviews with self-made millionaires and billionaires can provide valuable insights into their mindset, strategies, and habits that contributed to their success. Here are some potential questions you could ask during interviews with these individuals:

1. What motivated you to start your entrepreneurial journey, and how did you identify your initial business idea?

2. What were some of the biggest challenges you faced early on, and how did you overcome them?

3. How important was risk-taking in your path to success? Can you share a specific risk that paid off?

4. Many people fear failure. Can you share a failure or setback you experienced and how you bounced back from it?

5. What role did continuous learning and self-improvement play in your success? How do you stay updated and keep honing your skills?

6. How did you approach building and leading a successful team? What qualities do you look for in your team members?

7. Could you describe a pivotal moment or decision that significantly accelerated your business growth?

8. How do you manage your time and prioritize tasks to maximize productivity and efficiency?

9. What advice would you give to someone looking to start their own business or venture?

10. How do you handle competition and stay ahead in a constantly evolving market?

11. What role did networking and building relationships play in your journey? How do you approach networking effectively?

12. As your wealth grew, how did your approach to financial management and investing evolve?

13. Can you share an example of an innovative strategy or unique approach you took that set your business apart from others?

14. How do you balance work, personal life, and well-being to maintain a fulfilling lifestyle?

15. Looking back, what do you consider your most significant achievement, and what legacy do you hope to leave?

Remember that each individual's journey is unique, and their insights can offer valuable lessons and inspiration. Tailor your questions to the specific person you're interviewing and their areas of expertise. Listening to their experiences and learning from their successes and challenges can provide valuable guidance for aspiring entrepreneurs and individuals seeking to achieve financial success.

Lessons from Ordinary Individuals who Achieved Extraordinary Wealth

Lessons from ordinary individuals who achieved extraordinary wealth can offer valuable insights into the principles and practices that contributed to their success. Here are some key lessons that can be learned from their experiences:

1. Vision and Purpose:

- Many successful individuals had a clear vision of what they wanted to achieve. They set ambitious goals and worked diligently toward them with a strong sense of purpose.

2. Resilience and Persistence:
- Facing setbacks and challenges is common on the path to wealth. Those who persevered through difficulties, remained resilient, and kept pushing forward often saw their efforts pay off.

3. Continuous Learning:
- Lifelong learning was a common trait among those who achieved extraordinary wealth. They embraced new knowledge, sought out opportunities to expand their skills, and adapted to changing circumstances.

4. Smart Risk-Taking:
- Taking calculated risks was essential for many individuals. They made strategic decisions to seize opportunities, even when there was uncertainty involved.

5. Discipline and Hard Work:
- Extraordinary wealth often resulted from consistent and disciplined effort over time. Hard work, dedication, and a strong work ethic were frequently cited as contributing factors.

6. Creativity and Innovation:
- Many successful individuals found innovative solutions to problems or identified new market niches. They were open to creative thinking and explored uncharted territories.

7. Focus on Value Creation:
- Creating value for customers, clients, or the market was a recurring theme. Providing products or services that met a genuine need played a crucial role in their success.

8. Network and Relationships:
- Building strong relationships and networks helped open doors to opportunities, collaborations, and valuable insights.

9. Adaptability and Flexibility:
- Those who thrived in their pursuits were adaptable and willing to change course when needed. They recognized shifts in the market and adjusted their strategies accordingly.

10. Financial Savviness:
- Successful individuals understood the importance of managing finances wisely. They made informed investment decisions and took steps to protect and grow their wealth.

11. Giving Back:
- Many of these individuals believed in giving back to their communities or supporting charitable causes. Philanthropy was an integral part of their success story.

12. Long-Term Perspective:
- Extraordinary wealth often required a long-term perspective. Those who focused on

building sustainable growth rather than chasing short-term gains were more likely to achieve lasting success.

13. Embracing Failure as a Learning Opportunity:
- Those who achieved extraordinary wealth didn't let failure define them. Instead, they saw failures as opportunities to learn, adapt, and improve.

14. Empowerment and Self-Confidence:
- Self-confidence and the belief in their abilities played a crucial role in their success. They were not afraid to take ownership of their goals and decisions.

15. Personal Development:
- Many of these individuals invested in personal development, whether through self-help books, seminars, mentors, or coaches, to enhance their skills and mindset.

These lessons highlight the multifaceted qualities and actions that can contribute to achieving extraordinary wealth. While each individual's journey is unique, understanding and applying these principles can provide valuable guidance for anyone seeking to create a path toward financial success.

Actionable Takeaways from Real-Life Examples

Certainly, here are some actionable takeaways from real-life examples of individuals who achieved success and wealth:

1. Start with a Clear Vision:
- Define your goals and create a clear vision of what you want to achieve. Having a sense of direction will guide your actions.

2. Set Specific Goals:
- Break down your larger goals into smaller, actionable steps. This makes your journey more manageable and helps you track progress.

3. Embrace Failure as Learning:

- Don't let setbacks deter you. Use failures as opportunities to learn, adjust, and improve your strategies.

4. Continuous Learning:
- Invest in education and skill development. Acquire knowledge to stay relevant and adapt to changing circumstances.

5. Take Calculated Risks:
- Assess risks and rewards before making decisions. Strategic risk-taking can lead to innovation and growth.

6. Network and Build Relationships:
- Cultivate a strong network of connections. Building relationships can open doors to opportunities, collaborations, and insights.

7. Work Hard and Stay Persistent:
- Dedicate time and effort to your pursuits. Consistent hard work and persistence can yield significant results over time.

8. Focus on Value Creation:

- Prioritize creating value for others.
Providing solutions that meet needs is key to
attracting customers and clients.

9. Adapt to Change:
- Be willing to adapt to changing
circumstances and market trends. Flexibility
is essential for long-term success.

10. Manage Finances Wisely:
- Develop a sound financial plan, invest
strategically, and avoid unnecessary debt.

11. Stay Disciplined:
- Stick to your plans and remain disciplined
in managing your time, resources, and efforts.

12. Give Back:
- Consider how you can contribute to your
community or support causes you believe in.
Philanthropy can be rewarding and impactful.

13. Overcome Self-Doubt:
- Believe in your abilities and cultivate self-
confidence. Overcoming self-doubt can
empower you to take bold steps.

14. Innovate and Be Creative:
- Think outside the box and explore new approaches. Innovation can set you apart in competitive environments.

15. Find Passion and Purpose:
- Pursue ventures that align with your passion and values. Working on something meaningful can fuel your motivation.

Remember, these takeaways are not one-size-fits-all. Adapt them to your own circumstances, goals, and strengths. Learning from real-life examples can provide valuable guidance, but your journey is unique, and your actions should reflect your individual path to success.

In conclusion, achieving financial success and building wealth is a journey that requires a combination of strategic planning, disciplined actions, and a growth-oriented mindset. By understanding key financial concepts, adopting effective money management strategies, and learning from the experiences of self-made millionaires and billionaires, you can pave the way to a more secure and prosperous future.

From understanding the importance of financial education and budgeting to exploring various investment vehicles and managing debt, each step contributes to a solid foundation for financial well-being. Setting clear goals, managing risk, and developing a healthy relationship with money are essential aspects of achieving both short-term and long-term objectives.

In a rapidly changing world, adaptability is crucial. Embracing innovation, exploring entrepreneurship, and navigating economic shifts can open doors to new opportunities and avenues for growth. By learning from the successes and challenges of others, you can gain insights into how to turn crises into opportunities and capitalize on changing market dynamics.

Ultimately, the pursuit of financial success goes beyond monetary gains. It involves maintaining a work-life balance, focusing on well-being, and contributing positively to the world around you. By integrating these principles into your financial journey, you can create a path that not only leads to wealth but also to a fulfilling and meaningful life.

As you embark on this journey, remember that progress takes time, dedication, and a willingness to learn. Continuously educate yourself, seek guidance from professionals, and adapt your strategies as needed. With the right approach, you can build a strong financial foundation, overcome challenges, and achieve the financial success you aspire to.

www.ingramcontent.com/pod-product-compliance
Lightning Source LLC
Chambersburg PA
CBHW070849260726
48661CB00004B/1325